This Book Belongs TO:

PROJECT

COLORS:

ACCESSORIES

MATERIALS

PATTERNS

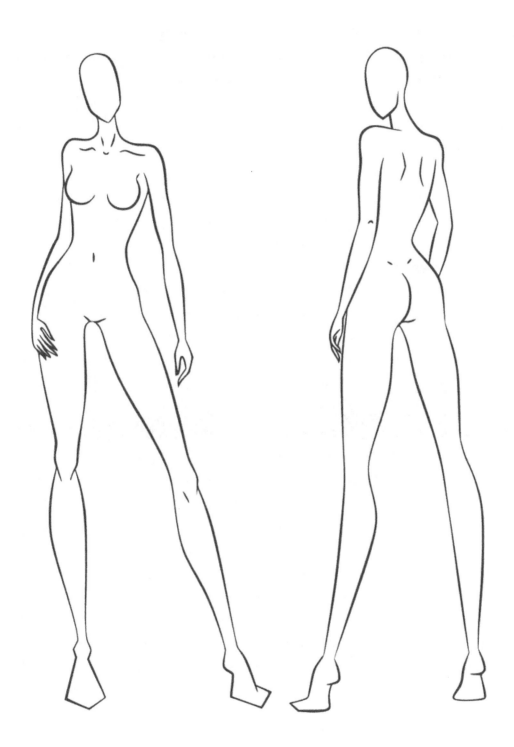

PROJECT

COLORS: ■ ☐ ☐ ☐ ☐ ☐ ☐ ☐ ☐ ☐ ☐ ☐ ☐

ACCESSORIES

MATERIALS

PATTERNS

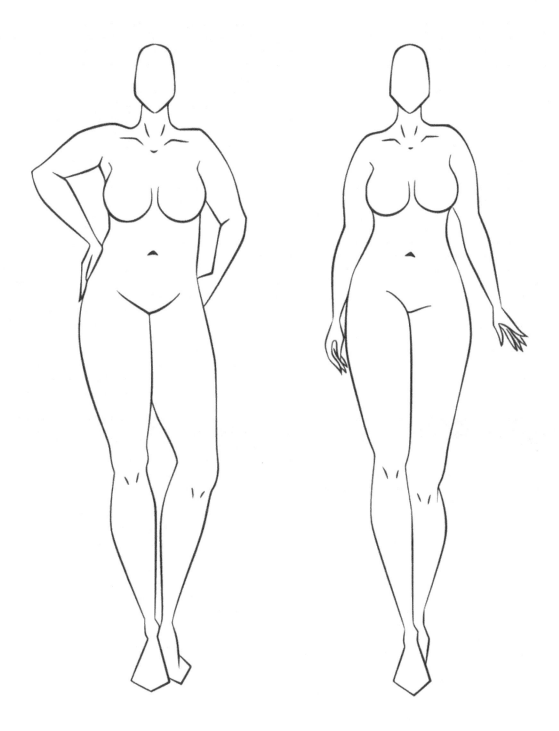

PROJECT

📅

COLORS: ⬛ ⬜ ⬜ ⬜ ⬜ ⬜ ⬜ ⬜ ⬜ ⬜ ⬜ ⬜ ⬜

ACCESSORIES

MATERIALS

PATTERNS

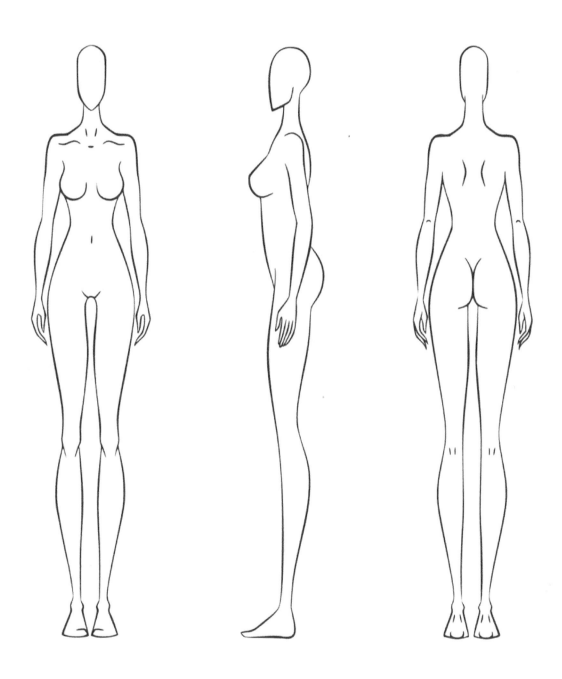

PROJECT

COLORS:

ACCESSORIES

MATERIALS

PATTERNS

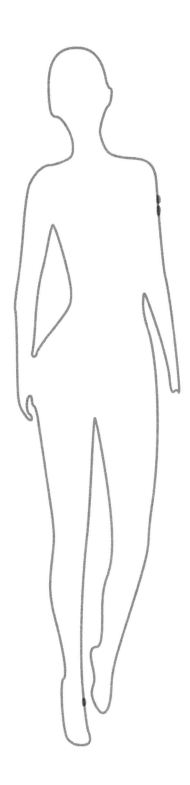

PROJECT

COLORS: ■ □ □ □ □ □ □ □ □ □ □ □ □

ACCESSORIES

MATERIALS

PATTERNS

PROJECT

COLORS:

ACCESSORIES

MATERIALS

PATTERNS

PROJECT

COLORS:

ACCESSORIES

MATERIALS

PATTERNS

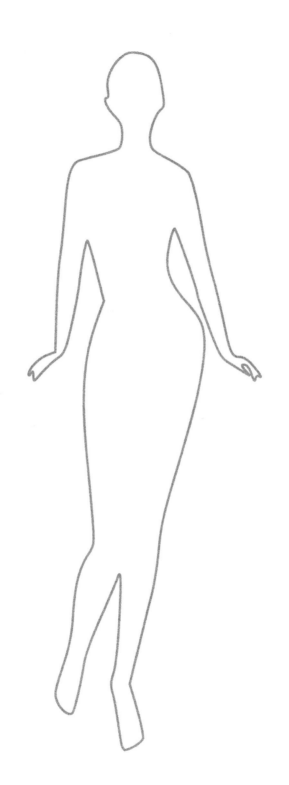

PROJECT

COLORS: ■ □ □ □ □ □ □ □ □ □ □ □ □

ACCESSORIES

MATERIALS

PATTERNS

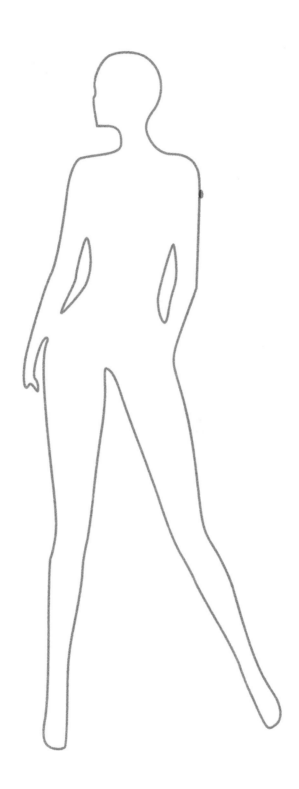

PROJECT

COLORS:

ACCESSORIES

MATERIALS

PATTERNS

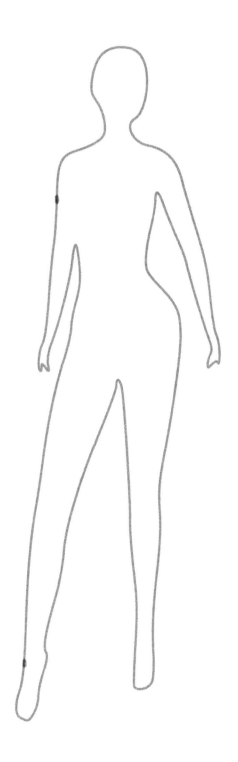

PROJECT

COLORS:

ACCESSORIES

MATERIALS

PATTERNS

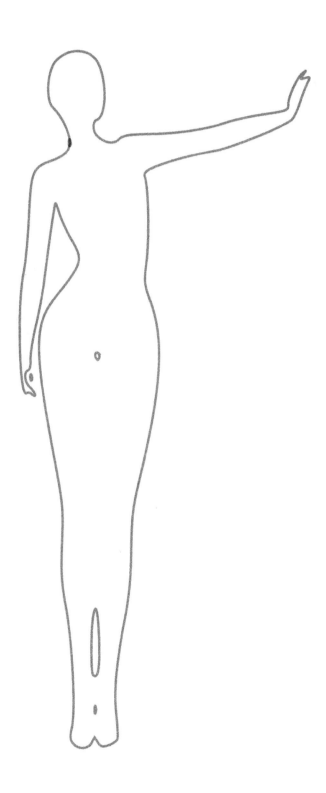

PROJECT

COLORS:

ACCESSORIES

MATERIALS

PATTERNS

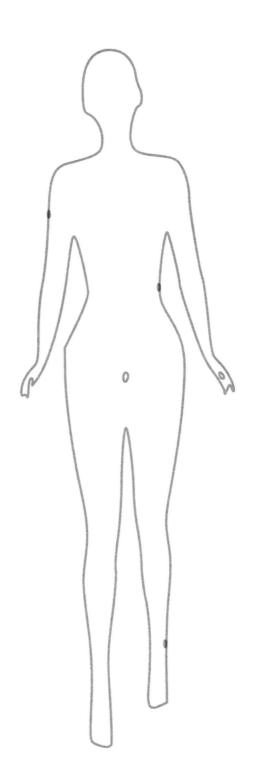

PROJECT	📅

COLORS: ■ □ □ □ □ □ □ □ □ □ □ □ □

ACCESSORIES

MATERIALS

PATTERNS

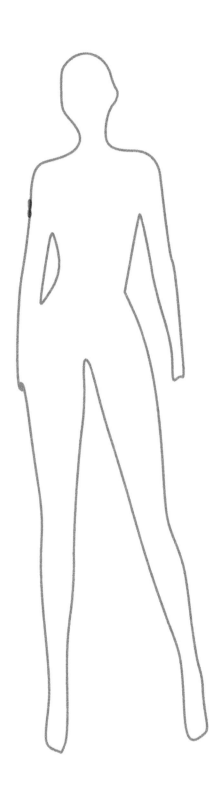

PROJECT

COLORS: ⬛ ⬜ ⬜ ⬜ ⬜ ⬜ ⬜ ⬜ ⬜ ⬜ ⬜ ⬜ ⬜

ACCESSORIES

MATERIALS

PATTERNS

PROJECT

COLORS:

ACCESSORIES

MATERIALS

PATTERNS

PROJECT

COLORS: ▪ ☐ ☐ ☐ ☐ ☐ ☐ ☐ ☐ ☐ ☐ ☐ ☐

ACCESSORIES

MATERIALS

PATTERNS

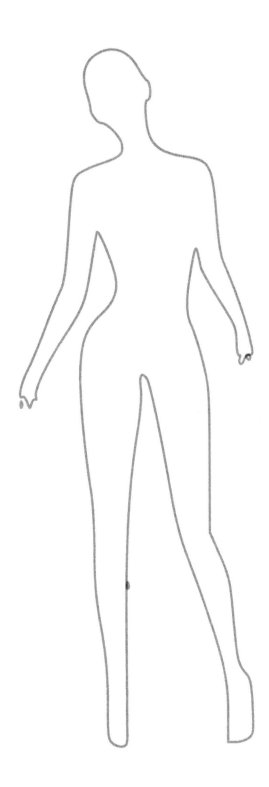

PROJECT

COLORS: ■ □ □ □ □ □ □ □ □ □ □ □ □

ACCESSORIES

MATERIALS

PATTERNS

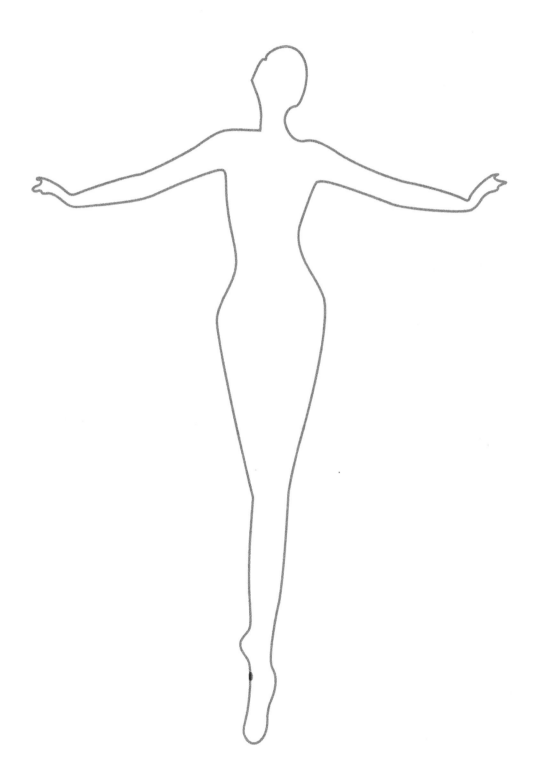

PROJECT

COLORS: ◼ ☐ ☐ ☐ ☐ ☐ ☐ ☐ ☐ ☐ ☐ ☐ ☐

ACCESSORIES

MATERIALS

PATTERNS

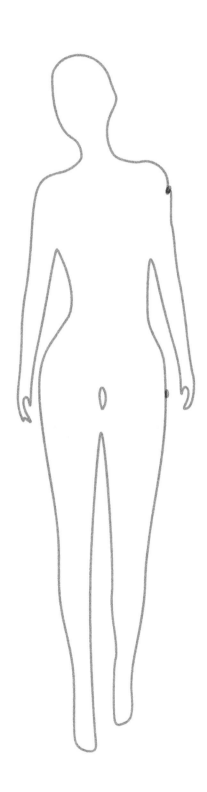

PROJECT	📅

COLORS: ■ □ □ □ □ □ □ □ □ □ □ □ □

ACCESSORIES

MATERIALS

PATTERNS

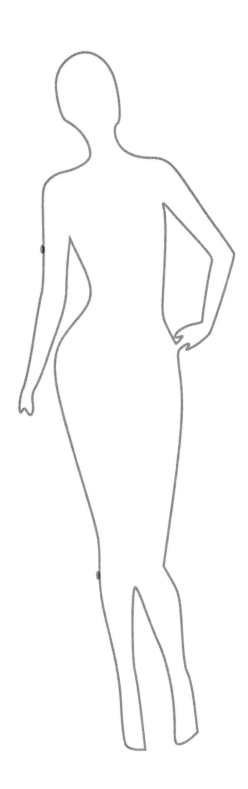

PROJECT

COLORS:

ACCESSORIES

MATERIALS

PATTERNS

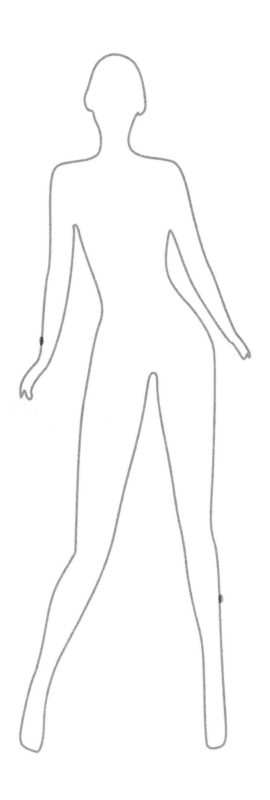

PROJECT

COLORS:

ACCESSORIES

MATERIALS

PATTERNS

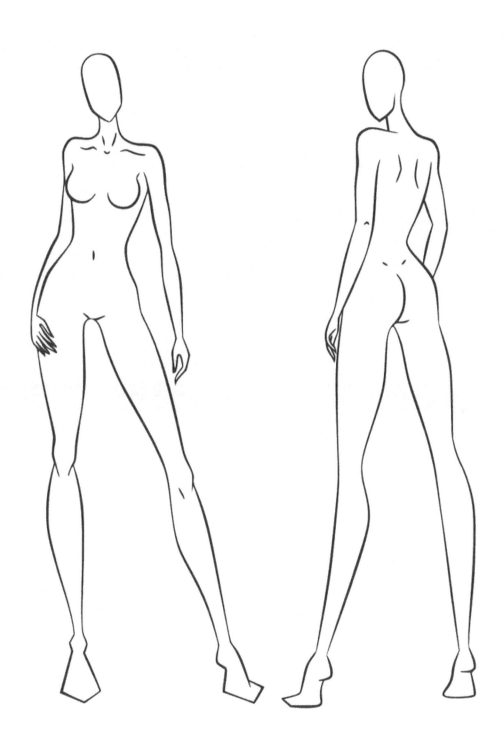

PROJECT

COLORS: ■ □ □ □ □ □ □ □ □ □ □ □ □

ACCESSORIES

MATERIALS

PATTERNS

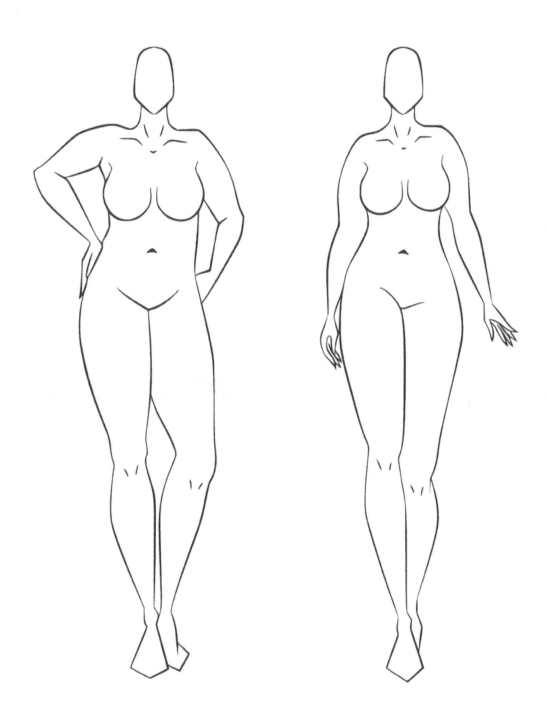

PROJECT

COLORS:

ACCESSORIES

MATERIALS

PATTERNS

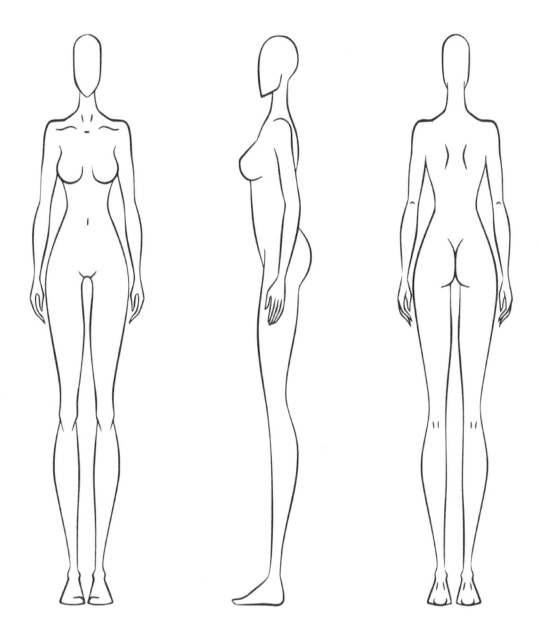

PROJECT

COLORS:

ACCESSORIES

MATERIALS

PATTERNS

PROJECT

COLORS:

ACCESSORIES

MATERIALS

PATTERNS

PROJECT

COLORS:

ACCESSORIES

MATERIALS

PATTERNS

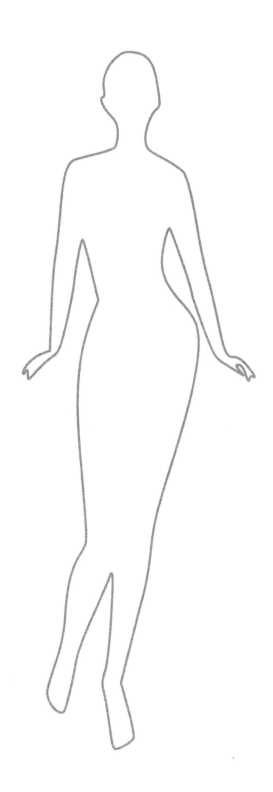

PROJECT

COLORS: ■ □ □ □ □ □ □ □ □ □ □ □ □

ACCESSORIES

MATERIALS

PATTERNS

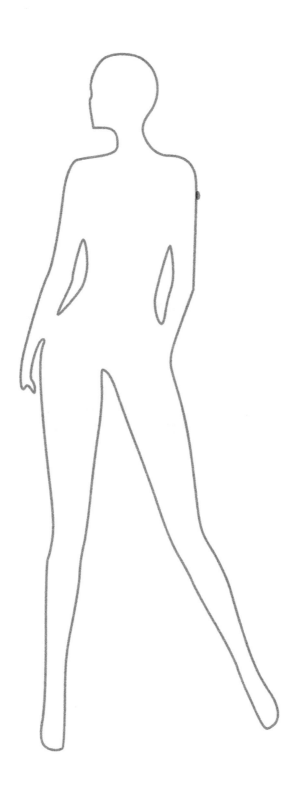

PROJECT

COLORS: ■ □ □ □ □ □ □ □ □ □ □ □ □

ACCESSORIES

MATERIALS

PATTERNS

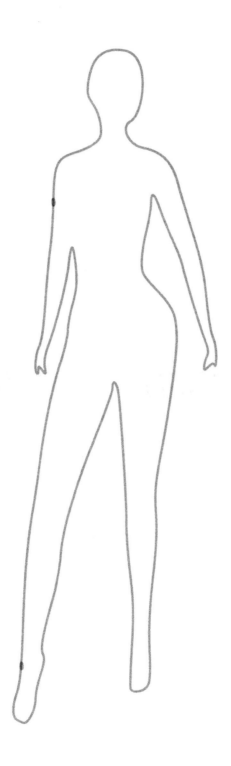

PROJECT

COLORS: ■ □ □ □ □ □ □ □ □ □ □ □ □

ACCESSORIES

MATERIALS

PATTERNS

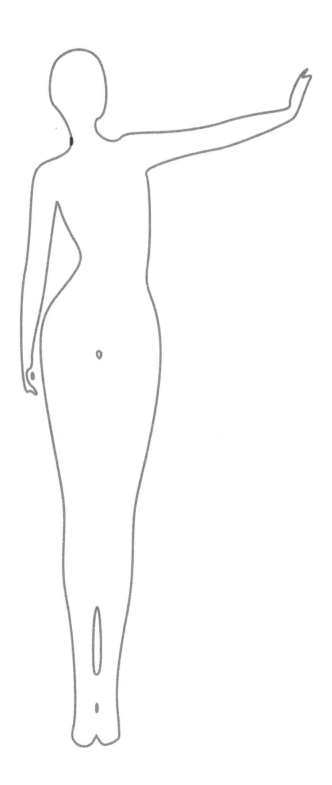

PROJECT

📅

COLORS: ⬛ ☐ ☐ ☐ ☐ ☐ ☐ ☐ ☐ ☐ ☐ ☐ ☐

ACCESSORIES

MATERIALS

PATTERNS

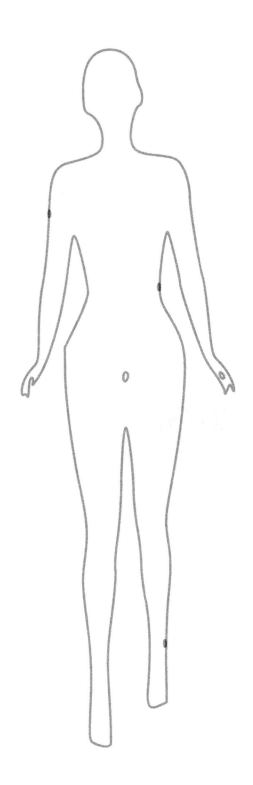

PROJECT

COLORS: ■ □ □ □ □ □ □ □ □ □ □ □ □

ACCESSORIES

MATERIALS

PATTERNS

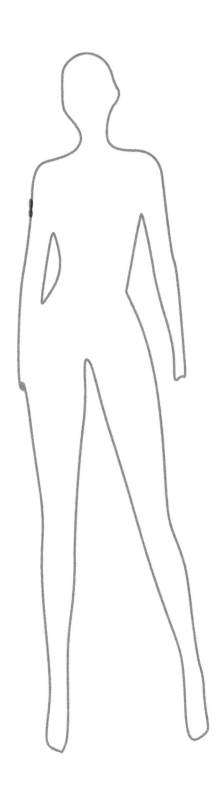

PROJECT

COLORS: ■ □ □ □ □ □ □ □ □ □ □ □ □

ACCESSORIES

MATERIALS

PATTERNS

PROJECT

COLORS:

ACCESSORIES

MATERIALS

PATTERNS

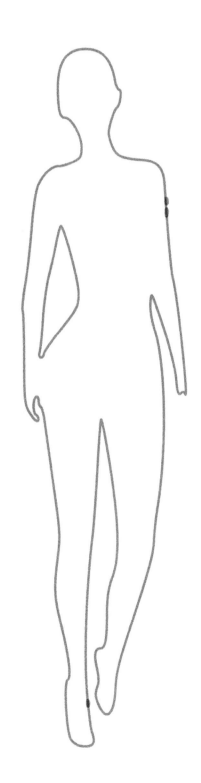

PROJECT

COLORS:

ACCESSORIES

MATERIALS

PATTERNS

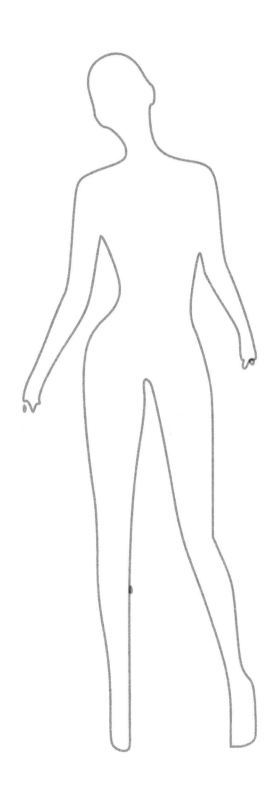

PROJECT

COLORS:

ACCESSORIES

MATERIALS

PATTERNS

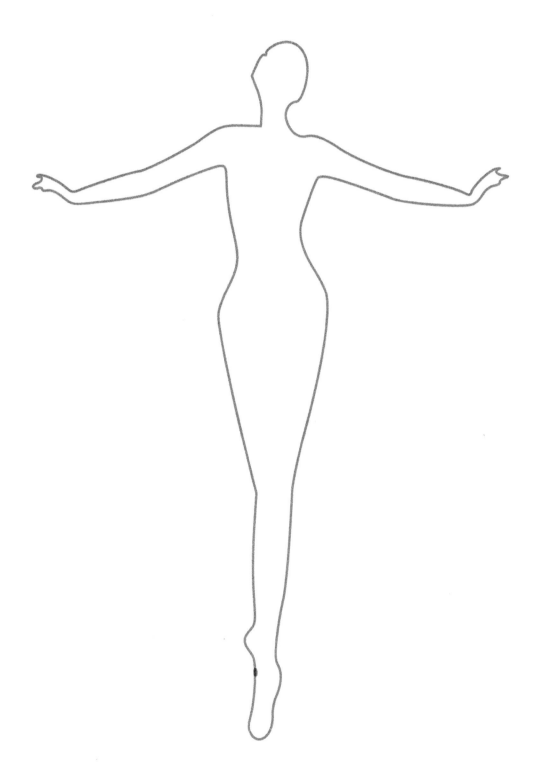

PROJECT

COLORS:

ACCESSORIES

MATERIALS

PATTERNS

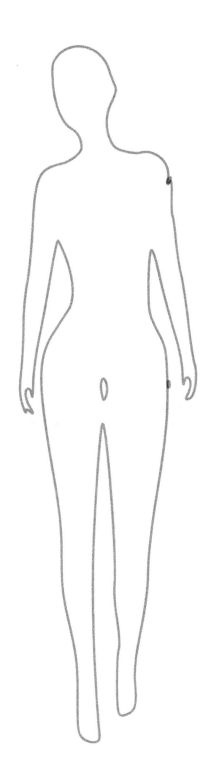

PROJECT

COLORS:

ACCESSORIES

MATERIALS

PATTERNS

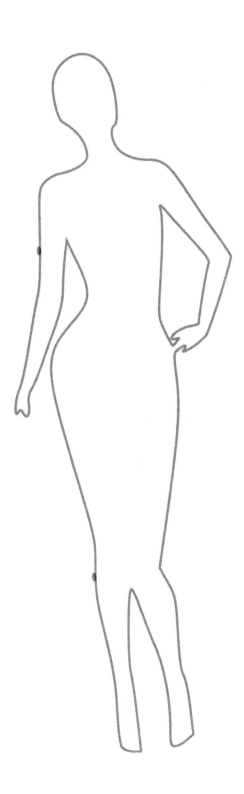

PROJECT

COLORS:

ACCESSORIES

MATERIALS

PATTERNS

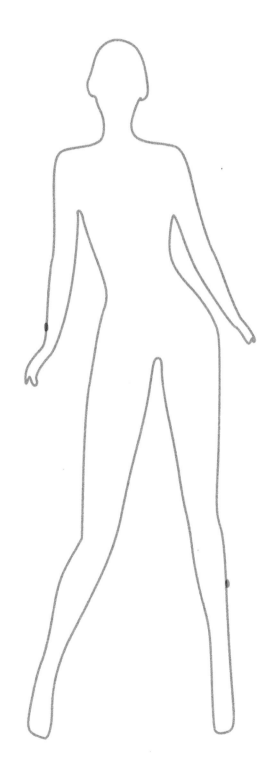

PROJECT

PROJECT

PROJECT

PROJECT

Notes

Notes

Notes

Notes

Notes

Notes

Thank you.

We would really appreciate your feedback. If you liked this book, please send us an email to:

magicalcolorspress@gmail.com

CPSIA information can be obtained
at www.ICGtesting.com
Printed in the USA
BVHW010829070621
608732BV00012B/1088